Mrs Woollylegs gets a haircut

It was hot. Very hot. Mrs Woollylegs stretched out on the grass to keep cool.

"Don't worry Mrs Woollylegs," said Mr Peach, Mrs Woollylegs' human. "Woollywashers are coming today."

The NewsSpaper

Mrs Woollylegs' ears pricked up. What did he mean, "WOOLLYWASHERS ARE COMING TODAY"? Before she had time to think, she heard a van pull up.

It was at that moment Mrs Woollylegs remembered she didn't like Woollywashers, so she bolted across the garden, knocking over Mr Peach's potted petunias on her way.

"Come back Mrs Woollylegs!" called Mr Peach desperately. "Woollywashers are here to give you a cooling bath and haircut!"

But Mrs Woollylegs wasn't listening. She kept on running, charging her way through the garden.

She ran so fast that she crashed through a hole in the fence into Mr Grumble's garden next door.

SH!

SQUELLLCCCHHH!!!! Mrs Woollylegs tumbled headfirst into the compost heap.

What on earth was that?!" cried Mr Grumble, looking p from his potato patch.

Mrs Woollylegs peered through a gap in the compost. She was covered from head to toe in mushy fruit and veg.

She shook her head and body as hard as she could to rid herself of rotting apples full of worms, soggy potat peelings, stinky tomatoes, slimy black banana skins and chunks of mouldy cabbage.

ithout warning, an apple core, which had been stuck her fur, was catapulted high into the air and landed slap bang in the face of Mr Grumble.

3leughhh!" shouted Mr Grumble crossly, wiping apple sludge from his cheeks.

But that wasn't all. Mrs Smart, Mr Grumble's prim and proper neighbour, suddenly poked her head over her perfectly pruned hedge. She was wearing a hat made of a banana skin and was looking angrily at Mr Grumble.

"Mr Grumble!" she shouted in disbelief. "How dare you throw your rotting compost into my garden!"

"It wasn't me! It was that nuisance of a dog from next door!" bellowed Mr Grumble, his face red with rage.

"You cause trouble wherever you go, dog!" snapped Mr Grumble. He was about to scold Mrs Woollylegs some more, but as he stared at Mrs Smart's squishy banana skin hat, a wicked smile crept over his face (which was still covered in apple sauce).

"Err... but, maybe you've been punished enough," he added. "Now trot off back home."

Mrs Woollylegs tiptoed back through the hole in the fence. Suddenly the idea of a bath and haircut didn't seem like such a bad idea...

So before too long, the van door opened and out trotted a happy, sparkling clean dog.

"There!" said Mr Peach. "Don't you look and smell jus like roses!"

Mrs Woollylegs felt fabulous.
The only thing was, she wasn't
Mrs Woollylegs anymore...

SHE WAS MRS SKINNYLEGS!

Printed in Great Britain
by Amazon

69226162R00015